BOOK ANALYSIS

Written by Clarisse Spies
Translated by Emma Hanna

The Swallows of Kabul

BY YASMINA KHADRA

YASMINA KHADRA — 11
Algerian writer

THE SWALLOWS OF KABUL — 15
Surviving in the midst of violence

SUMMARY — 19
A nightmarish setting
Realisation dawns
The descent into hell
The ultimate sacrifice

CHARACTER STUDY — 29
Atiq Shaukat
Mussarat Shaukat
Mohsen Ramat
Zunaira Ramat
Qassim Abdul Jabbar
Mirza Shah
Nazeesh

ANALYSIS — 39
The war in Afghanistan
Devastation
The image of the couple
Loneliness and a lack of communication

FURTHER REFLECTION — 53

Some questions to think about...

FURTHER READING 57

YASMINA KHADRA

ALGERIAN WRITER

- **Born in Kenadsa (Algerian Sahara) in 1955.**
- **Notable works:**
  - *The Attack* (2005), novel
  - *What the Day Owes the Night* (2008), novel
  - *The Dictator's Last Night* (2015), novel

Yasmina Khadra is the pseudonym of Mohammed Moulessehoul, who created the pen-name using his wife's two forenames. His father was a nurse who worked with the ALN (National Liberation Army of Algeria) and his mother was a nomad. Khadra was born in 1955 and studied at a military academy before embarking on a military career that spanned 36 years, during which he reached the rank of major.

After initially publishing under his own name, he began using pseudonyms from 1989 onwards and eventually left the army in 2000 in order to devote himself to his career as a writer. In 1997 he published *Morituri*, the first novel in his series centred on the Police Superintendant Brahim Llob, under the pseudonym Yasmina Khadra, which brought him to widespread public attention. After a short stay in Mexico with his wife and three children, he settled in Aix-en-Provence in France in 2001, and still lives there today.

He has received many literary awards during his career, in particular for *The Swallows of Kabul*, which was awarded the Prix du salon littéraire de Metz and the Prix des libraires algériens in 2003, was voted best book of the year by two American newspapers (the *San Francisco Chronicle* and the *Christian Science Monitor*) in 2005, and was shortlisted for the IMPAC Dublin Literary Award in 2006.

THE SWALLOWS OF KABUL

SURVIVING IN THE MIDST OF VIOLENCE

- **Genre:** novel
- **Reference edition:** Khadra, Y. (2005) *The Swallows of Kabul*. Trans. Cullen, J. London: Vintage.
- **1ˢᵗ edition:** 2002
- **Themes:** Afghanistan, war, oppression, despair, women's rights, loneliness, the Taliban

This novel tells the story of two couples who are trying to survive in Kabul, which has been devastated by war and over which the Taliban regime rules with an iron fist. Atiq Shaukat is a former *mujahideen* (jihadist fighter) turned prison guard, and now oversees prisoners who have been sentenced to death. He lives with his wife Mussarat, who is terminally ill. Mohsen Ramat, a once-wealthy man, is simply trying to survive along with his beloved wife Zunaira, a former lawyer who has lost the right to practise due to the introduction of sharia law. As the story unfolds, these four characters witness tragedy after tragedy, including public executions, the loss of rights, and food shortages. Day by day, their hopes of seeing their dreams of modernity and freedom restored slip further and further away.

SUMMARY

A NIGHTMARISH SETTING

The novel opens with a description of a Kabul that seems to have risen from the depths of hell, which is in the clutches of the Taliban and ruled by sharia law: the heat is unbearable, and the surrounding lands have been devastated by war, rendered barren and grotesque. "And yet it is also here, amid the hush of stony places and the silence of graves [...] that our story is born, like the water lily that blooms in a stagnant swamp" (p. 3).

Atiq Shaukat is hurrying to the prison where he works as a guard: a public execution is due to take place, and he is running late because his wife Mussarat, who is terminally ill, had to be taken to the hospital urgently. Her illness is taking a toll on him, but he cannot bring himself to abandon her, because she saved his life many years ago. He somehow manages to cross the city to collect the prisoner: a woman caught having an affair who is to be stoned. He finds Qassim

Abdul Jabbar, a low-level Taliban officer, waiting to receive the prisoner.

We meet Mohsen Ramat, a formerly affluent businessman who loathes violent spectacles, at the scene of the execution. Despite his distaste, he gets caught up in the emotionally charged atmosphere and takes part in the stoning. He is immediately riddled with guilt and shame for giving in to this impulse.

REALISATION DAWNS

Atiq leaves the prison with no idea where he should go: he is plagued by unease as he rushes through the streets that swarm with beggars, traders and orphans. Where should he go? His uncle is half-mad, his wife is ill and he wants nothing more than a moment of peace. He cannot understand why he survived fighting in the wars only to live in this broken world ruled by fundamentalists. As he takes a detour down a side street, he bumps into Mirza Shah, his childhood friend with whom he was reunited when they fought together as *mujahideens* during the early days of the Russian invasion.

Mohsen returns home to Zunaira, his wonderful wife, with whom he lives in perfect harmony. She is a former lawyer who is unable to practise because of the new regime which bans women from working. Filled with shame, he confesses that he took part in a public stoning. Zunaira cannot accept or move past this, and the couple is plunged into a downward spiral.

The next day, Atiq goes to the mosque at the call to prayer. In the courtyards, he watches as old men exchange stories about their military exploits with those who were wounded in the wars. Eventually, he returns home, where he discovers that Mussarat has left herself utterly exhausted after getting up, cleaning and preparing a meal for him. Despite this, they argue, and Atiq leaves the house. He decides to sleep in the camp bed in his tiny office at the prison. While he is there, Nazeesh, a poor, half-mad old man, comes to visit him and brings him something to eat. Nazeesh talks about his dream of packing his bags and leaving the city, never to return, to escape the horrors of Kabul. Atiq cruelly tells him that he will never do it and the two men part after this argument.

Atiq does not understand why he has become so cruel. He picks arguments with everyone for no good reason. He feels as though he has changed, as though all hope has been taken from him. The next day, he goes to apologise to Nazeesh, who nevertheless ends up scaling the rocks, in spite of his advanced age, to leave Kabul for good.

THE DESCENT INTO HELL

Zunaira and Mohsen have reconciled, and decide to take a walk through the city, like they used to before the dictatorship took control of it. Zunaira, who has stopped going out since wearing the burqa, a traditional Afghan garment which covers the entire body, was made compulsory for women, decides to wear this loathsome piece of clothing so that she can go out for a walk with her husband and make him happy.

However, they have not gone far when the Taliban militia forces Mohsen to attend a sermon at the mosque. Zunaira is made to wait outside the building, suffocating in her burqa. The prayer seems to last an eternity, and when they return home, Zunaira has changed: she refuses to take off the burqa, she will not speak to her husband,

and she does not even want to look at him.

Mohsen cannot bear his wife's silence any longer: "For ten days, Mohsen has lived in a state of total infirmity, in a delirium worthy of King Ubu" (p. 126). He returns home and tries to talk to her once again, but the argument turns ugly, and Mohsen suffers a fatal fall.

Shortly afterwards, Atiq, who is still feeling overwhelmed by despair and plagued by his torments, greets a militiaman at the prison who announces that a new prisoner will be arriving soon: it is Zunaira, who has been condemned to death. Later that afternoon, Qassim arrives with the prisoner as the clamour of a battle rings out in the background. She will remain under guard for several days before being executed in front of a large crowd which will include several high-ranking individuals. A dozen executions will be carried out in the stadium as entertainment during that gathering.

Once he is alone with Zunaira, he watches over her, and it is not long before he is utterly captivated by her beauty. It has been a long time since he last gazed upon the face of any woman other than Mussarat, as they are all imprisoned within their burqas: "flocks of infirm swallows" (p. 121), as he calls them. It is as though Zunaira has bewitched him, and Mussarat notices that something has changed within him. He feels well, after being plagued by a constant despair for so long. He tells Mussarat about the prisoner's arrival, her beauty and his fascination with her, and Mussarat is pleased to see that her husband is finally starting to feel something again. She even suggests preparing some food for the woman who has brought a spark of life back to her husband.

Atiq and Zunaira talk over the course of the following days. The jailer soon realises that she is not guilty and that it was all an accident. He imagines all the possible ways that she could be saved from paying the ultimate price. He even opens the cell door to let Zunaira escape, but she remains immovable:

> "'I won't let them kill you.' 'We've all been killed, all of us. It happened so long ago, we've forgotten it'" (p. 164).

THE ULTIMATE SACRIFICE

Mussarat eventually realises that Atiq is in love with the prisoner. She is delighted by this, as she sees that her husband has finally been freed of his constant anguish and is able to love again. As Atiq is returning to the prison for a few last moments with Zunaira before her execution at dawn the next morning, Mussarat appears unexpectedly. She has come up with a plan: she will take Zunaira's place, since she is doomed to die of her illness anyway. No one will notice any difference because of the burqa covering her face and body. Zunaira will wait in Atiq's office, pretending to be his wife, and will then leave. Atiq therefore goes to find Zunaira and lies to her, telling her that she has been pardoned and that she must wait in his office.

After that, everything happens very quickly: Qassim Abdul Jabbar comes looking for the prisoner, and then brings his family, as well as Atiq's wife – who is, of course, none other than Zunaira in disguise – to the stage to watch the executions. Atiq gives Zunaira some advice: to wait for him at the exit to the stadium, and then they will leave. But when the "festivities" are over, he cannot find her. He searches for her everywhere, before losing his grip on his sanity. He wanders as far as the graveyard to find Mussarat's tomb, then returns to the city. His scarred face and torn clothes make him look like a madman. He frightens the women and children, and it is not long before the men get involved, and blows begin raining down upon him from every direction. Atiq closes his eyes as the mob engulfs him and dies from his wounds, hoping that "his sleep may be as unfathomable as the secrets of the night" (p. 195).

CHARACTER STUDY

ATIQ SHAUKAT

Atiq is 42 years old and is a jailer in one of Kabul's prisons. He takes no pleasure in his job: he was once a brave *mujahideen* fighter, and he is merely surviving as best he can through a job built on tedium, loneliness and death. He is in "a state of constant rage [...] he feels as though he were burying himself alive" (p. 18).

20 years ago he married Mussarat, who had treated his wounds and saved his life during a battle. Atiq is a man burdened by his pain. While he used to be a sensitive soul, he has developed "a strange aggressiveness, imperious and unfathomable, which seems to fit his moods" (p. 87).

Atiq is completely transformed by his encounter with Zunaira: his fascination with her seems to revitalise him and fill him with hope. When he realises that Mussarat can save her, he has a fleeting glimpse of a potential fresh start. But after the execution, he is reduced to a mere shadow of himself, burdened by the guilt of causing his wife's death and alienated now that he has lost Zunaira, who has vanished.

MUSSARAT SHAUKAT

Mussarat is Atiq's terminally ill wife. She met her husband when his squad was defeated by the communist forces. She sheltered him in her village and tended to his wounds, putting her own life at risk to do so. Because of this, their marriage is more a symbol of Atiq's gratitude than a real love match. Mussarat is not pretty, is even showing early signs of baldness, and is aware that she does not have long to live. In spite of her troubles, she tries her best to play the role of a loving wife by keeping the house in order and preparing meals when she is able.

Mussarat is aware that her marriage is a loveless one in which communication has broken down completely. She does her best to "deserve [Atiq] at all costs" (p. 57), but never succeeds in making herself attractive to him. Because of this, when she realises that her husband has found joy and freedom again after meeting Zunaira in the prison, she decides to sacrifice her own life for the sake of his happiness.

MOHSEN RAMAT

Mohsen was born into the Afghan middle class, and was a prominent businessman before the war. But the war has taken everything away from him, and all he has left is his wife Zunaira, whom he met at university. The love they share is the only thing that gives him the strength to survive, and even though the couple's lives have been thrown into utter turmoil, they still have hope because of that love.

But as the novel progresses, Mohsen loses the love that gives his life meaning – first when he admits to Zunaira that he participated in a public stoning, and then later, after their walk is interrupted by the Taliban, when she no longer feels anything but bitter loathing towards any figure of male authority. At that point, "he thinks he's going mad" (p. 123). Unfortunately, during a last-ditch attempt to reason with Zunaira, he falls and hits his head on a carafe, which kills him and dooms his wife to a terrible fate. In the end, the war takes everything he has left: his wife, and his life.

ZUNAIRA RAMAT

Zunaira is an educated 32-year-old woman who became a lawyer after she graduated from university, and used to be a tireless activist for women's rights. She is uncommonly beautiful, and a loving, attentive wife. The fact that she can no longer work because of the Taliban causes her great pain, but she endures it, and she and her husband have never given up hope of living a better, more modern life in the future. She even refuses to leave the house for the sake of her principles, because she does not want to wear the burqa, and she cannot leave the house without it: "Don't ask me to become something less than a shadow, an anonymous thing rustling around in a hostile place" (p. 78).

Unfortunately, when the militia forces her to wait for her husband outside the mosque, having forced Mohsen himself to attend a sermon, something changes within her: "Zunaira perceives that disgust quite clearly: it's an inner ferment, it sears her guts and threatens to consume her like a burning pyre" (p. 99). From that moment on, she is consumed by rage and cannot stand to be in the presence of any man. After Mohsen's death, she is sentenced to death and ends up in Atiq's jail before vanishing in the wake of Mussarat's execution. Defeated by the war, she is already dead inside.

QASSIM ABDUL JABBAR

Qassim, Atiq's boss, is a low-level Taliban leader. Proud and remorseless, he never fails to carry out any task that is assigned to him. He is a brave fighter and a talented militiaman with small-scale ambitions: he dreams of becoming the director of the sinister Pul-e-Sharki prison in order to rise through the ranks until he has enough public standing to launch a career in business. He adheres to the law blindly with absolutely no regard for sentimentality: he has many wives, and returns to Kabul immediately after burying his mother instead of remaining in his village.

He is the embodiment of a fanatical underling: one of the system's tools, malleable and selfish, who sows fear everywhere he goes and is proud to do so. When he meets Atiq, he sums up his life's philosophy for him:

> "If you start from the assumption that existence is only an ordeal, a test we have to pass, then you're equipped to deal with its sorrows and surprises. If you persist in expecting it to give you something it can't give, that just proves that you haven't understood anything" (p. 118).

MIRZA SHAH

Mirza is a childhood friend of Atiq's and a devoted *mujahideen*. They were reunited when they fought together during the war. Mirza has refused to take any position that comes with responsibilities since the Soviet troops withdrew, preferring to make his living through all kinds of trafficking and smuggling. He is bribing the authorities, which means that he can live comfortably in the eye of the storm. An advocate of polygamy, he tries to convince Atiq to abandon Mussarat to make his life easier. He is among those who have accepted and adjusted to life under the newly established Taliban regime, and does not hesitate to criticise women and consider them inferior.

He has no thoughts of rebellion and is not consumed by despair; he is satisfied with the way things are and acts accordingly. "We've always lived this way. One king left; another divinity replaced him. [...] Some people waste their time waiting to see a new era dawning on the horizon" (p. 25).

NAZEESH

Nazeesh is a man in his 60s with a gaunt face. He used to be a *mufti* (an Islamic scholar) who ranked among the most important people in Kabul. The war has taken his sons and his wits from him. Nowadays he looks on in apathy as the days go by, half-mad and yearning for the past, and for the singing and dancing which were a symbol of joy, but which are now forbidden in Kabul. He spends his time claiming that he is going to pack his bags and leave, but no one believes him. He personifies the inner chaos that each character faces. Fleeing is the only way to find hope: in the end Nazeesh does leave, and is the only character to escape this living hell.

> "He wants to go to the country he's seen in fantastic daydreams, the one he's built with his sighs and his prayers and his dearest wishes – a country where the trees don't die of boredom,

> where the paths wander and drift like birds, where no one will look askance on his resolve to journey to the immutable lands from which he will never return" (p. 106).

ANALYSIS

THE WAR IN AFGHANISTAN

The novel takes place against the backdrop of the war which broke out in Afghanistan at the end of the 1970s.

The first stage of the war, which lasted for ten years, between 1979 and 1989, saw the USSR face off against the *mujahideens*. Soviet forces invaded the country to support the PDPA (People's Democratic Party of Afghanistan), which was attempting to enact Marxist reforms which ran contrary to Afghanistan's conservative traditions (women's rights, literacy, a secular state, etc.), and sought to crush all traces of Islamic opposition to the ruling communist regime. Muslim resistance, in the form of the *mujahideen* army, soon rose up to oppose the Soviet invaders, and received significant support from the CIA, the United States, and the West. After years of fighting and negotiations, the Soviet forces withdrew in 1989 under orders from Mikhail Gorbachev (Russian statesman, born 1931).

At this point, the war in Afghanistan entered a second stage. After the retreat of the Soviet forces, a civil war soon broke out between the *mujahideens*, who were backed by the United States, and the Afghan army, which had been formed by the communist government and which was still supplied by weapons left by the Soviet troops. The communist regime held the upper hand for a while, until the USSR was no longer able to keep providing them with the promised supplies of food, fuel and weapons. As such, Kabul was recaptured by the *mujahideens* in 1992.

After the Soviet troops withdrew in 1989 and the communist regime collapsed in 1992, the various Afghan political parties signed the Peshawar Accord (24 April 1992), which established the Islamic State of Afghanistan. However, the Accord was not respected, and conflict broke out between various factions of the *mujahideens*, eventually leaving Kabul drained of resources and plunging the city into poverty and devastation.

From 1994 onwards, the Taliban movement swiftly gained strength. This faction was determined to free the country from all the fighting it was embroiled in and to establish a government based on the application of sharia law. The Taliban was supported by the population, who were tired of the wars. After several bloody battles, the Taliban took control of Kabul in 1996 and imposed sharia law strictly and violently. Even so, the civil war raged on.

This is the Kabul that Atiq, Mussarat, Mohsen and Zunaira live in – a deadly city ruled by the whims of the Taliban.

DEVASTATION

The theme of devastation can be seen at various levels of the novel. Firstly, in terms of the city, through descriptions which are strongly linked to the senses of sight and smell. Secondly, in terms of the crowd that throngs the streets of Kabul, with the way that its inhabitants' spirits have been crushed by the war being conveyed through their physical appearance and their behaviour.

The devastation of Kabul

From the very beginning of the novel, Kabul is portrayed as a city devastated by conflict. The "post"-war period has not given rise to peace and rebuilding; on the contrary, the choice of words here conveys how the Taliban regime is perpetuating a system of oppression:

> "The cratered roads, the scabrous hills, the white-hot horizon, the pinging cylinder heads all seem to say, *Nothing will ever be the same again*. The ruin of the city walls has spread into people's souls. The dust has stunted their orchards, blinded their eyes, sealed up their hearts." (p. 2)

The words used here refer in equal measure to inanimate features of the city (roads, orchards, etc.) and to the people who live there (eyes, hearts). Here, the author is describing a kind of no-man's land which is both the physical result of the battles and a metaphorical representation of the population's spirits, as most of them have been impoverished and oppressed.

The vocabulary used throughout the novel to describe this ruined city and its defeated inhabitants plays on the reader's senses of sight, smell and hearing: "the stench of animal carcasses" (p. 2), "the emanations of rotting produce" (p. 5), "red stain" (p. 14), "a dissonant chorale" (p. 19), "foul-smelling basins" (p. 20), "squealing" and "shouts" (p. 22), etc. In this way, the reader is immersed in this city, which is only a shadow of its former self, through their senses, and they can feel for themselves how much these ruins repulse the characters.

Heat is another recurring theme in the vocabulary used in the novel, creating a chaotic, desert-like atmosphere:

> "The calcified palm trees thrust against the sky like beseeching arms." (p. 1)
> "And all around him, there's the exceedingly arid landscape. It's as though the land has despoiled itself in order to heighten the distress of those who live there, trapped between the rocks and the blazing heat. The sparse strips of greenery that deign to show themselves here and there make no promise of blooming; the blades of the baked grass crumble at the least quiver. Like gigantic dehydrated hydras, the streams languish in their undone beds, with nothing but their stony bowels to offer to the sunstroke gods." (p. 112)

Here, the descriptions of nature convey the sense of utter hopelessness, as hope is like a plant which will never again be able to take root in such a barren, hellish landscape.

The desperate crowd

The theme of devastation also manifests itself through the crowds that haunt Kabul's streets. The city's inhabitants are everywhere, not just at public events but also surrounding the main characters when they are walking or wandering through the streets. This crowd is described in a fairly pejorative way, which is a metaphorical representation of the hopeless living hell that the city has become. As such, a tremendous number of beggars and orphans gleaning whatever food they can find appear in the novel, and are often so persistent that they will only be moved by blows from a whip. Many disabled ex-soldiers also appear, gathering in front of the mosque in an attempt to win back their former prestige by recounting the daring military feats that they took part in. The Taliban militiamen are generally described as having scarred faces and dirty, untidy clothes, while the militiawomen are shrouded in their burqas and the traders hawk their rotten produce. This is an anonymous crowd, but it is a perfect reflection of the atmosphere that the characters are living in: after all, how can they make sense of their lives or find a glimmer of hope when they are surrounded by such figures?

> "The shopkeepers have put their smiles in the storeroom. The chilam smokers have vanished into thin air. The men of Kabul have taken cover behind shadow puppets, and the women, mummified in shrouds the color of fever or fear, are utterly anonymous." (p. 11)

Certain characters personify different aspects of this anonymous crowd: for example, Qassim, the fundamentalist militiaman who upholds the regime; Nazeesh, whose nostalgic longing for change eventually drives him to flee the city; and Mirza Shah, the cynic who adapts to anything life throws at him.

Public events and prayers are now the only things that bring people together. A kind of frenzy takes hold of the crowd during public executions, which are organised for the simple purpose of sowing fear and thus consolidating the Taliban's rule of terror, although they also serve to entertain the masses like in the age of the gladiators: as the saying goes, *panem et circenses* (bread and games).

> "The prestigious guests, who are coming to share the joy of public executions; the notables, who will applaud the implementation of the Sharia [...] Including Kabul itself, the accursed city, every day more expert in killing, more dedicated to the opposite of living. In this land, the public celebrations have become as appalling as the lynchings themselves." (p. 160)

THE IMAGE OF THE COUPLE

The main characters of this story are two couples: Atiq and Mussarat, and Mohsen and Zunaira. These two couples have a symbolic meaning that goes far beyond that of people who are merely trying to survive.

Atiq and Mussarat's marriage follows the customs of their conservative culture; in other words, theirs is a loveless marriage, but it conforms to Islamic precepts. Atiq married Mussarat because she helped him, which was more a sign of gratitude than anything else. Atiq's authority gradually relegated Mussarat to a subservient role, and she also lives with a constant, nagging guilt due in particular to her illness and her infertility ("'I want to perform my wifely duties until the end'"; "'I feel that I must be failing in my obligations as a wife'" p. 53). This shows that Mussarat has been indoctrinated by the backwards teachings of the most tyrannical religious leaders, who insist that women must submit to their husbands and be obedient to them. This couple seems to look semi-favourably upon the Taliban regime, believing it to have been established for the good of the Afghan people in the wake of so many wars. The author presents them as fairly unattractive, weak and sickly.

The couple formed by Mohsen and Zunaira is completely different to the first couple in every way. These two characters married for love, and are young, attractive and educated. They are utterly opposed to the Taliban regime, as they view the new laws as primitive and an infringement on their freedom. Zunaira, who is a university graduate, no longer has the right to work or to go outside without wearing a burqa. She sees the Taliban as oppressors who have no sense of justice and who have tried to take away her humanity: "If I put that damned veil on, I'm neither a human being nor an animal, I'm just an affront, a disgrace, a blemish that has to be hidden" (p. 78). Mohsen has lost his business and has had to sell his belongings in order to survive. He, too, dreams of a future built on modernity and justice. However, both of them reluctantly obey the new laws in order to avoid punishment, while hoping that change will come in time.

The author seems to use the couples' physical appearance as a way of conveying his own opinions: the first couple, who support the regime, are quite ugly and sickly; the second couple, who are progressive and in favour of gender equality, are young and attractive. As such, the reader could potentially associate Atiq and Mussarat with "evil" and Mohsen and Zunaira with "good". But things are not completely black and white: Mohsen goes against all his principles to take part in a stoning, while Atiq rediscovers his humanity when he falls in love.

LONELINESS AND A LACK OF COMMUNICATION

Throughout the novel, the characters frequently withdraw into themselves in a kind of selective mutism. The passers-by drive the beggars out of their way using whips, which have become the nation's "official language" (p. 124). Women are hidden away inside their burqas. Laughing in the street and listening to the radio are no longer permitted. Everyone is categorically cut off from each other and from the rest of the world.

Things are no different for the couples: Atiq prefers to avoid his wife and his home, sleeping at the prison and storming out of his house after the slightest disagreement: "'My husband doesn't speak to me anymore. [...] Since we have a chance to talk for once [...] let's try not to quarrel'" (pp. 53-54). In fact, Atiq can no longer bear to interact with anyone at all, avoiding all communication and locking himself away in his fortress of solitude: "I can't bear the dark, I can't bear the light, I don't like standing up or sitting down, I can't tolerate old people or children, I hate it when anybody looks at me or touches me. In fact, I can hardly stand myself. Am I going stark raving mad?" (p. 42).

As for Mohsen and Zunaira, after the incident during their walk, they both isolate themselves even more, each in their own way: "Zunaira has withdrawn into an overwhelming silence [...] When he leaves his house, he hastens to the old cemetery, where he spends hours and hours alone" (p. 112).

The reader naturally draws the conclusion that the relationships within the novel suffer from a lack of communication. Each of the characters is free in theory, but is actually a prisoner of the Taliban regime, of the ruins of Kabul, of loss and of poverty. This reinforces the loneliness each person feels and spreads it through the entire city. None of the characters seem truly able to make their words heard: no one believes old Nazeesh when he says he is going to leave, Zunaira's complaints are never met with a response, and the pleas of the beggars in the street go utterly ignored.

The characters are even incapable of listening to themselves: "Mohsen's former points of reference have all disappeared, and he hasn't got the strength to invent any new ones. [...] Reduced to the ranks of the untouchables, he spends his days stagnating, always deferring until later the promise to pull himself together" (p. 79).

FURTHER REFLECTION

SOME QUESTIONS TO THINK ABOUT...

- Read Mullah Bashir's sermon on pages 93 to 97. What do you think of his teachings? Do you agree with him? Why?
- Give two examples of personification in the novel. In your opinion, what effect does that create?
- Who are the "swallows of Kabul"? Why was that chosen as the title?
- Why is the condemned woman stoned at the start of the book? What is your opinion of this practice?
- Comment on this quote describing Kabul: "It's a chaos within chaos, a disaster enclosed in disaster, and woe to those who are careless" (p. 71).
- In your opinion, what are the reasons for Zunaira's anger towards her husband? Explain your answer.
- Which of the novel's characters do you identify

with most? If you were in their position, how would you react to their misfortunes?
- Who are the *mujahideens*? Why do they fight?
- What are the differences between the Taliban and the *mujahideens*?
- Comment on this quote from Mussarat: "'In this country, there are many mistakes but never any regrets. The question of execution or mercy, of death or life, isn't resolved by deliberation. No, such decisions are made according to the whim of the moment'" (p. 175).

We want to hear from you!
Leave a comment on your online library
and share your favourite books on social media!

FURTHER READING

REFERENCE EDITION

- Khadra, Y. (2005) *The Swallows of Kabul*. Trans. Cullen, J. London: Vintage.

ADAPTATIONS

- *The Swallows of Kabul*. (2019) [Film]. Zabou Breitman and Eléa Gobbé-Mervellec. Dir. France: Les Armateurs.
- *Les Hirondelles de Kaboul*. (2013) [Play]. Jean-Louis Wacquiez. Dir. France: Compagnie Nomades.
- *Les Hirondelles de Kaboul*. (2010) [Play]. Antoinette Senior. Dir. France/Turquie/Brazil/Ecuador: Vue Sur Scène.

MORE FROM BRIGHTSUMMARIES.COM

- Reading guide – *What the Day Owes the Night* by Yasmina Khadra.

Bright ≡Summaries.com

More guides to rediscover your love of literature

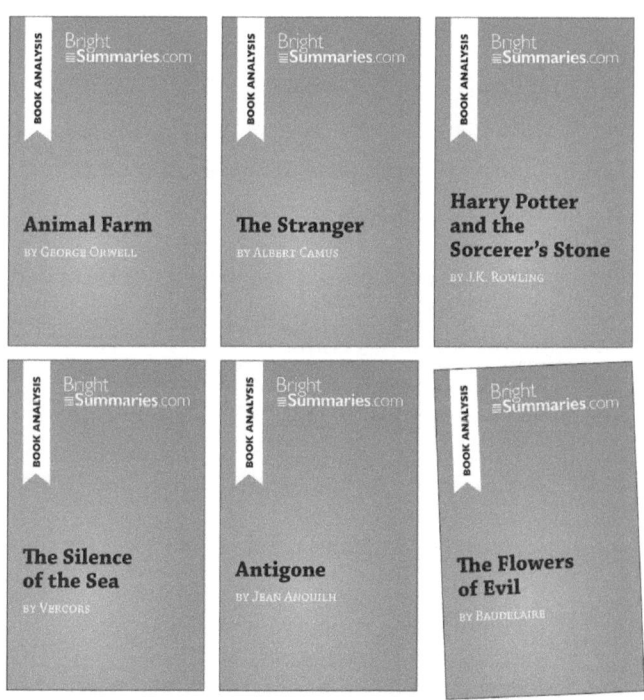

www.brightsummaries.com

Although the editor makes every effort to verify the accuracy of the information published, BrightSummaries.com accepts no responsibility for the content of this book.

© BrightSummaries.com, 2016. All rights reserved.

www.brightsummaries.com

Ebook EAN: 9782808004381

Paperback EAN: 9782808004398

Legal Deposit: D/2017/12603/749

Cover: © Primento

Digital conception by Primento, the digital partner of publishers.